SARAH MITCHELL

DBT Workbook For Autism

Navigating Emotions and Thriving with Dialectical Behavior Therapy

Contents

1 Chapter 1   1

  Introduction   3

    About This Workbook   3

    How to Use This Workbook   4

    What is Dialectical Behavior Therapy (DBT)?   4

    How DBT Can Help Individuals with Autism   6

2 Chapter 2   8

  Understanding Emotions   8

    Recognizing Emotions   9

    Understanding the Function of Emotions   9

    Identifying Primary and Secondary Emotions   10

    Emotion Regulation Strategies   10

3 Chapter 3   13

  Mindfulness   13

    What is Mindfulness?   14

    Mindfulness Skills for Individuals with Autism   14

4 Chapter 4   18

  Distress Tolerance   18

    Coping with Intense Emotions   19

    Crisis Survival Skills   20

5 Chapter 5   23

  Interpersonal Effectiveness   23

    Building and Maintaining Relationships   24

6 Chapter 6   28

Core Mindfulness   28
  Observing, Describing, and Participating   29
  Non-judgmental Stance   30
  One-mindfully   31
  Effectively   32
7 Chapter 7   34
  Emotion Regulation   34
    Understanding Emotion Regulation   35
    Strategies for Managing Emotions   35
    Identifying Triggers and Vulnerabilities   36
8 Chapter 8   39
  Walking the Middle Path   39
    Balancing Acceptance and Change   40
    Finding Middle Ground   41
    Radical Acceptance   42
    Finding Meaning and Purpose   43
9 Chapter 9   45
  Putting It All Together   45
    Review of Skills Learned   45
    Creating a Personalized DBT Plan   46
    Moving Forward with Confidence   48
  Conclusion   49

1

Chapter 1

A Personal Exploration of DBT and Autism

Every morning, I woke up feeling overwhelmed by the intense emotions swirling inside me. Dealing with the intricacies of everyday life was a struggle for me as a young adult with autism. Sensory overload, social challenges, and emotional dysregulation were constant companions on my journey.

Determined to find a way to manage my emotions and live a more fulfilling life, I decided to enroll in a Dialectical Behavior Therapy (DBT) program. Each day, I embarked on a journey of self-discovery and growth, guided by the principles and techniques of DBT.

In the beginning, mindfulness practices felt foreign to me. Sitting still and focusing on my breath seemed impossible amidst the chaos of my racing thoughts. But with patience and persistence, I began to notice small moments of calm and clarity emerging from the noise.

As I delved deeper into DBT, I learned strategies for identifying and regulating my emotions. I practiced labeling my feelings, recognizing triggers, and implementing coping skills to navigate moments of distress. Gradually, I gained a sense of mastery over my emotions, finding solace in the midst of chaos.

Interpersonal effectiveness was another area where I struggled. Social interactions often left me feeling confused and misunderstood. But through role-playing exercises and assertiveness training, I learned to communicate my needs and boundaries with confidence and clarity. As a result, my relationships with friends and family blossomed, and I felt a newfound sense of connection and belonging.

One of the most transformative aspects of my journey was learning to embrace radical acceptance. Instead of fighting against my autism or wishing things were different, I learned to accept myself exactly as I was – quirks, challenges, and all. This radical acceptance freed me from the burden of self-criticism and allowed me to embrace my unique strengths and gifts.

With each passing day, I felt myself growing stronger and more resilient. I no longer saw my autism as a limitation, but rather as a source of strength and resilience. Armed with the tools and insights gained from DBT, I faced life's challenges with courage and conviction, knowing that I had the power to create a life filled with meaning, purpose, and joy.

As I reflected on my journey, I felt an overwhelming sense of gratitude for the transformative power of DBT. It had not only helped me manage my emotions and navigate the complexities of autism, but it had also empowered me to embrace my true self and live authentically in the world.

Introduction

The journey towards understanding and managing emotions, building healthier relationships, and achieving a sense of balance and stability can be challenging for individuals with autism. This workbook aims to provide a comprehensive guide to Dialectical Behavior Therapy (DBT) techniques specifically tailored to the needs of individuals on the autism spectrum. By combining evidence-based strategies with insights into the unique experiences of autism, this workbook offers practical tools and exercises to promote emotional regulation, improve communication skills, and enhance overall well-being. Whether you're navigating the complexities of daily life, seeking to strengthen relationships, or simply looking to better understand yourself, this workbook is designed to support you every step of the way.

About This Workbook

This workbook serves as a companion on your journey to emotional well-being and personal growth. Through a combination of psychoeducation, experiential exercises, and reflection, this workbook aims to empower individuals with autism to develop greater self-awareness, emotional resilience, and interpersonal effectiveness. The content is presented in a user-friendly format, with clear instructions and examples to guide you through each exercise. Additionally, this workbook includes worksheets and handouts that can be used to reinforce learning and track progress over time.

How to Use This Workbook

To make the most of this workbook, it is recommended to work through each chapter sequentially, starting with chapter 1 and progressing through to chapter 8. Take your time with each exercise, allowing yourself the space to explore and practice new skills at your own pace. While some exercises may feel challenging at first, remember that progress is incremental, and each step you take brings you closer to your goals. Feel free to adapt the exercises to suit your individual needs and preferences, and don't hesitate to seek support from a therapist or trusted individual if needed. Above all, approach this workbook with an open mind and a willingness to engage with the material, knowing that you have the capacity to cultivate positive change in your life.

What is Dialectical Behavior Therapy (DBT)?

Dialectical Behavior Therapy (DBT) is a form of cognitive-behavioral therapy that was originally developed by Dr. Marsha Linehan to treat individuals with borderline personality disorder (BPD). However, DBT has since been adapted to address a wide range of mental health concerns, including depression, anxiety, substance use disorders, and eating disorders. Central to DBT is the concept of dialectics, which emphasizes the synthesis of seemingly contradictory ideas or perspectives. In DBT, this dialectical approach is applied to the balance between acceptance and change, acknowledging the need to both accept oneself as you are while also striving for growth and improvement.

DBT is comprised of four primary modules, each targeting specific areas of skill development:

- **Mindfulness**: Mindfulness skills help individuals cultivate awareness of their thoughts, emotions, and sensations in the present moment without judgment. By practicing mindfulness, individuals can learn to observe their experiences with greater clarity and respond more effectively to life's challenges.
- **Distress Tolerance**: Distress tolerance skills teach individuals how to cope with intense emotions and crises without resorting to harmful behaviors. These skills include distraction techniques, self-soothing strategies, and crisis survival skills to help individuals navigate difficult situations with greater resilience.
- **Emotion Regulation**: Emotion regulation skills focus on identifying and managing emotions in healthy and adaptive ways. Through emotion regulation techniques, individuals can learn to understand the function of their emotions, identify triggers and vulnerabilities, and develop strategies for modulating emotional intensity.
- **Interpersonal Effectiveness**: Interpersonal effectiveness skills help individuals navigate social interactions and build

healthier relationships. These skills include effective communication, assertiveness training, and setting boundaries to promote mutual respect and understanding in relationships.

How DBT Can Help Individuals with Autism

While DBT was originally developed for individuals with borderline personality disorder, its principles and techniques can be beneficial for individuals with autism as well. Autism is characterized by difficulties with social communication and interaction, as well as restricted interests and repetitive behaviors. As a result, individuals with autism may struggle with emotional regulation, interpersonal relationships, and managing stress and anxiety.

DBT offers a structured and systematic approach to addressing these challenges, providing practical tools and strategies for enhancing emotional awareness, communication skills, and coping abilities. By learning to recognize and regulate their emotions, individuals with autism can experience greater stability and well-being in their daily lives. Additionally, DBT helps individuals develop interpersonal skills that are essential for building and maintaining meaningful relationships, both within their personal and professional lives.

One of the key strengths of DBT is its emphasis on validation and acceptance, which can be particularly beneficial for individuals with autism who may have experienced feelings of rejection or misunderstanding. Through DBT, individuals with autism can learn to accept themselves as they are while also working

6

towards personal growth and development. By embracing the dialectical balance between acceptance and change, individuals with autism can cultivate a greater sense of self-compassion and resilience in the face of life's challenges.

2

Chapter 2

Understanding Emotions

E motions are complex psychological and physiological responses that play a fundamental role in human experience. They provide valuable information about our internal states, alerting us to our needs, desires, and responses to the world around us. Emotions encompass a wide range of feelings, from joy and love to sadness, anger, fear, and everything in between. For individuals with autism, understanding emotions can be particularly challenging due to differences in social communication, sensory processing, and emotional regulation. Many individuals with autism may have difficulty recognizing and interpreting facial expressions, body language, and other nonverbal cues that convey emotional information. As a result, they may struggle to identify and express their own emotions or understand the emotions of others.

Recognizing Emotions

Recognizing emotions involves being able to identify and label the various feelings that arise within oneself and others. This includes recognizing the physical sensations, facial expressions, vocal tones, and behavioral cues associated with different emotions. For individuals with autism, who may have differences in sensory processing and social communication, recognizing emotions can be a complex and nuanced process. They may rely on alternative strategies, such as focusing on specific features of facial expressions or using visual aids, to help them recognize and interpret emotions more effectively. Additionally, individuals with autism may benefit from explicit instruction and practice in emotion recognition skills, including identifying emotions in photographs, videos, or social stories.

Understanding the Function of Emotions

Emotions serve important adaptive functions, helping us to navigate our social interactions, make decisions, and respond to our environment. For example, fear alerts us to potential threats, while joy motivates us to seek out rewarding experiences. Understanding the function of emotions involves recognizing the purpose behind each emotion and how it influences our thoughts, behaviors, and decision-making processes. Individuals with autism may benefit from psychoeducation and cognitive-behavioral interventions that help them understand the role of emotions in their lives and how to respond to them adaptively. By understanding the function of emotions, individuals with autism can gain insight into why they may be experiencing certain emotions in particular situations and how they can effectively respond to them.

Identifying Primary and Secondary Emotions

Emotions are often complex and multifaceted, involving both primary and secondary components. Primary emotions are the initial, instinctual responses to a stimulus, such as fear in response to a perceived threat or joy in response to a positive experience. Secondary emotions, on the other hand, are the additional layers of emotional experience that arise in response to our thoughts and interpretations of a situation. For example, feeling angry about feeling sad or feeling guilty about feeling angry are examples of secondary emotions. Individuals with autism may benefit from learning to identify and differentiate between primary and secondary emotions, as this can help them understand the underlying factors influencing their emotional experiences. By recognizing the interconnected nature of emotions, individuals with autism can develop more nuanced emotional regulation strategies and enhance their emotional well-being.

Emotion Regulation Strategies

Emotion regulation refers to the ability to effectively manage and modulate one's emotional experiences. For individuals with autism, who may experience heightened emotional sensitivity or difficulty regulating their emotions in response to sensory stimuli, learning effective emotion regulation strategies is essential for promoting emotional well-being. There are several strategies that individuals with autism can use to regulate their emotions:

- **Mindfulness Practices**: Mindfulness techniques, such as deep breathing, meditation, and body scanning, can help individuals with autism become more aware of their emotions and physical sensations in the present moment. By practicing mindfulness, individuals can learn to observe their emotions without judgment and respond more intentionally and calmly to challenging situations.
- **Cognitive Restructuring**: The process of cognitive restructuring entails recognizing and combating maladaptive or erroneous thought patterns that fuel unpleasant feelings. Individuals with autism can benefit from cognitive-behavioral interventions that help them recognize and reframe negative thoughts, reducing emotional distress and improving their overall mood.
- **Emotion Expression**: Finding healthy outlets for expressing emotions can help individuals with autism process and release pent-up feelings in a constructive manner. This may include journaling, creative expression, or engaging in physical activities that allow for emotional release.
- **Self-Soothing Techniques**: Self-soothing techniques, such as listening to calming music, engaging in sensory activities, or practicing relaxation exercises, can help individuals with autism regulate their emotions and reduce stress and anxiety in overwhelming situations. These techniques provide individuals with a sense of comfort and safety, allowing them to manage their emotions more effectively.
- **Social Support**: Seeking support from trusted friends, fam-

ily members, or therapists can provide individuals with autism with validation, empathy, and guidance in navigating their emotional experiences. Building a support network of people who understand and accept them can help individuals with autism feel more connected and supported in managing their emotions.

By incorporating these and other emotion regulation strategies into their daily lives, individuals with autism can enhance their emotional resilience, reduce emotional distress, and improve their overall quality of life. While learning to regulate emotions may take time and practice, individuals with autism have the capacity to develop valuable skills that enable them to navigate their emotional experiences with greater ease and confidence.

3

Chapter 3

Mindfulness

Mindfulness is a practice rooted in ancient Buddhist traditions that has gained popularity in contemporary psychology as a powerful tool for promoting well-being and reducing stress. Fundamentally, mindfulness is accepting, inquiring, and paying attention to the current moment. Rather than dwelling on the past or worrying about the future, mindfulness encourages individuals to cultivate awareness of their thoughts, emotions, bodily sensations, and surrounding environment in the here and now. For individuals with autism, who may experience heightened sensory sensitivity and difficulty regulating their emotions, mindfulness can offer valuable skills for promoting emotional regulation, reducing anxiety, and enhancing overall quality of life.

What is Mindfulness?

Mindfulness is often defined as the practice of intentionally bringing one's attention to the present moment without judgment. This involves becoming aware of one's thoughts, emotions, bodily sensations, and surroundings with an attitude of curiosity, openness, and acceptance. Mindfulness can be cultivated through formal meditation practices, such as mindfulness of breath or body scan meditation, as well as through informal practices, such as mindful eating or walking. By developing mindfulness skills, individuals can learn to respond to life's challenges with greater clarity, resilience, and compassion.

Mindfulness Skills for Individuals with Autism

For individuals with autism, who may experience sensory overload, difficulty with social communication, and heightened emotional sensitivity, mindfulness can offer a range of benefits. Mindfulness skills can help individuals with autism become more attuned to their internal experiences, allowing them to better regulate their emotions and respond more effectively to stressors. Additionally, mindfulness can enhance self-awareness and self-acceptance, fostering a greater sense of calm and well-being. Some mindfulness skills that may be particularly beneficial for individuals with autism include:

1. **Sensory Awareness**: Mindfulness encourages individuals to become more aware of their sensory experiences, including sights, sounds, smells, tastes, and tactile sensations. For individuals with autism, who may have heightened sen-

14

sory sensitivity or difficulty filtering out irrelevant stimuli, mindfulness can help them develop greater awareness and acceptance of their sensory experiences.

2. **Emotion Regulation**: Mindfulness practices teach individuals to observe their emotions without judgment and to respond to them with compassion and acceptance. By cultivating a non-reactive stance towards their emotions, individuals with autism can learn to regulate their emotional responses more effectively and reduce emotional distress.

3. **Body Awareness**: Mindfulness practices often involve bringing attention to the sensations present in the body, such as tension, discomfort, or relaxation. For individuals with autism, who may experience challenges with body awareness and motor coordination, mindfulness can help them develop greater sensitivity to their bodily sensations and cultivate a sense of embodied presence.

4. **Social Mindfulness**: Mindfulness can also be applied to social interactions, helping individuals with autism become more attuned to the thoughts, feelings, and needs of others. By practicing mindful listening and compassionate communication, individuals with autism can improve their social skills and enhance their relationships with others.

Practicing Mindfulness in Daily Life While formal meditation practices are an important aspect of mindfulness training, mindfulness can also be integrated into daily life through informal practices. Some ways to incorporate mindfulness into daily life include:

1. **Mindful Breathing**: Taking a few moments to focus on the

sensation of the breath as it enters and leaves the body can help anchor attention in the present moment and promote relaxation.

2. **Mindful Eating**: Paying attention to the sensory experience of eating, such as the taste, texture, and smell of food, can enhance enjoyment and satisfaction while also promoting mindful eating habits.

3. **Mindful Walking**: Bringing awareness to the sensations of walking, such as the feeling of the ground beneath the feet and the movement of the body, can help ground individuals in the present moment and promote a sense of embodied presence.

4. **Mindful Activities**: Engaging in everyday activities with mindfulness, such as washing dishes, brushing teeth, or taking a shower, can help individuals cultivate presence and attention in their daily routines.

Mindfulness Exercises and Activities There are a variety of mindfulness exercises and activities that individuals with autism can practice to develop their mindfulness skills. Some examples include:

1. **Body Scan Meditation**: This involves systematically scanning through the body from head to toe, bringing attention to any sensations or areas of tension or relaxation.

2. **Breathing Meditation**: Focusing on the breath as it moves in and out of the body, noticing the rise and fall of the abdomen or the sensation of air passing through the nostrils.

3. **Sensory Awareness Practice**: Engaging in activities that bring attention to each of the five senses, such as mindful

listening to music, mindful tasting of food, or mindful touching of different textures.

4. **Nature Meditation**: Spending time in nature and bringing awareness to the sights, sounds, smells, and sensations of the natural world can promote relaxation and a sense of connection to the environment.

5. **Loving-Kindness Meditation**: This involves cultivating feelings of compassion and goodwill towards oneself and others, sending wishes for happiness, health, and well-being to oneself, loved ones, and even to strangers or difficult individuals.

By incorporating mindfulness into their daily lives and practicing mindfulness exercises regularly, individuals with autism can develop valuable skills for promoting emotional regulation, reducing stress and anxiety, and enhancing overall well-being. Mindfulness is not a cure-all solution, but rather a practice that requires patience, persistence, and self-compassion. With continued practice and dedication, individuals with autism can cultivate greater presence, awareness, and resilience in the face of life's challenges.

4

Chapter 4

Distress Tolerance

D istress tolerance is a crucial skill for navigating life's inevitable challenges and setbacks. It involves the ability to tolerate and withstand intense emotions, distressing situations, and crises without resorting to harmful or self-destructive behaviors. For individuals with autism, who may experience heightened emotional sensitivity and difficulty regulating their emotions, distress tolerance skills can be particularly valuable. By learning effective coping strategies and building resilience in the face of adversity, individuals with autism can develop greater emotional stability, reduce impulsivity, and enhance their overall quality of life.

Coping with Intense Emotions

Coping with intense emotions is a key aspect of distress tolerance. When faced with overwhelming feelings such as anger, sadness, or anxiety, it's important to have healthy coping mechanisms in place to help manage and regulate those emotions. For individuals with autism, who may experience emotional dysregulation or difficulty identifying and expressing their feelings, coping with intense emotions can be especially challenging. However, there are several strategies that can help individuals with autism cope more effectively with intense emotions:

- **Identify Triggers**: Recognize the situations, thoughts, or experiences that tend to trigger intense emotions, and develop strategies for managing these triggers when they arise.
- **Practice Self-Awareness**: Learn to recognize the physical and emotional signs of distress, such as racing heart, tense muscles, or racing thoughts, and take proactive steps to address these symptoms before they escalate.
- **Use Grounding Techniques**: Grounding techniques, such as deep breathing, progressive muscle relaxation, or focusing on the present moment, can help individuals with autism stay anchored and centered during moments of emotional distress.
- **Seek Support**: Reach out to trusted friends, family members, or therapists for support and validation during times of emotional turmoil. Talking about your feelings with others can help you gain perspective and feel less alone in your struggles.

Crisis Survival Skills

Crisis survival skills are essential for managing acute moments of distress or crisis. These skills help individuals with autism stay safe and navigate challenging situations without resorting to harmful or impulsive behaviors. Some crisis survival skills that individuals with autism may find helpful include:

- **Creating a Safety Plan**: Develop a plan for how to stay safe during moments of crisis, including identifying supportive individuals to contact, creating a list of coping strategies, and knowing when to seek professional help or intervention.
- **Using Distress Tolerance Techniques**: Practice distress tolerance techniques, such as self-soothing strategies, distraction techniques, and mindfulness exercises, to help regulate emotions and reduce distress during crisis situations.
- Seeking Professional Help: If you're experiencing a crisis and are unable to cope on your own, don't hesitate to reach out to a therapist, counselor, or crisis hotline for support and guidance. It's important to know that you're not alone and that help is available.

Distracting Techniques

Distracting techniques can help individuals with autism shift their focus away from distressing thoughts or emotions and engage in more adaptive and enjoyable activities. These techniques can be particularly helpful during moments of intense emotional distress or when facing overwhelming situations. Some distracting techniques that individuals with autism may find helpful include:

- **Engaging in Hobbies**: Participate in activities that you enjoy and find relaxing, such as drawing, playing music, or gardening. Engaging in hobbies can help distract your mind from distressing thoughts and promote a sense of accomplishment and well-being.
- **Physical Exercise**: Engage in physical activities, such as walking, running, or yoga, that help release pent-up energy and promote relaxation. Physical exercise can also stimulate the release of endorphins, which are natural mood-lifters.
- **Mindful Distraction**: Practice mindful distraction by focusing your attention on the present moment and engaging fully in whatever activity you're doing. This could involve focusing on the sensations of your breath, the sights and sounds around you, or the physical sensations of movement.

Self-Soothing Strategies:

Self-soothing strategies help individuals with autism calm and comfort themselves during moments of distress or emotional upheaval. These strategies can be particularly helpful for individuals who struggle with emotional regulation or sensory sensitivities. Some self-soothing strategies that individuals with autism may find helpful include:

- **Sensory Comfort**: Use sensory tools or objects, such as fidget toys, weighted blankets, or calming music, to provide comfort and regulate sensory input during moments of distress.
- **Self-Compassion**: Practice self-compassion by offering yourself kindness and understanding during times of difficulty. Remind yourself that it's okay to feel upset or overwhelmed, and treat yourself with the same kindness

and compassion that you would offer to a friend in need.

- **Creating a Safe Space**: Create a designated safe space where you can retreat to when feeling overwhelmed or distressed. This could be a quiet room, a cozy corner with soft blankets and pillows, or a favorite outdoor spot where you feel calm and grounded.
- **Engaging the Senses**: Use sensory-based self-soothing techniques, such as aromatherapy, warm baths, or gentle massage, to provide comfort and relaxation during moments of distress. Try out a variety of sensory experiences to see which suits you the best.

By incorporating these distress tolerance skills, coping strategies, distracting techniques, and self-soothing strategies into their daily lives, individuals with autism can enhance their emotional resilience, reduce distress, and improve their overall well-being. It's important to remember that building distress tolerance skills takes time and practice, and it's okay to seek support from others when needed. With patience, persistence, and self-compassion, individuals with autism can develop valuable tools for navigating life's challenges with greater ease and resilience.

5

Chapter 5

Interpersonal Effectiveness

Interpersonal effectiveness refers to the ability to navigate social interactions and build healthy, satisfying relationships with others. For individuals with autism, who may experience challenges with social communication, understanding social cues, and interpreting the thoughts and feelings of others, developing interpersonal effectiveness skills can be particularly valuable. By learning effective communication strategies, assertiveness techniques, and boundary-setting skills, individuals with autism can enhance their social competence, build meaningful connections, and cultivate more fulfilling relationships in their personal and professional lives.

Building and Maintaining Relationships

Building and maintaining relationships requires effort, communication, and mutual respect. For individuals with autism, who may struggle with social skills and understanding social norms, developing and sustaining relationships can be challenging. But with effort and assistance, people with autism can learn how to manage social situations more skillfully and form deep relationships with others. Some tips for building and maintaining relationships include:

- **Seeking Common Interests**: Look for shared interests and activities that you can enjoy together with others. Finding common ground can help strengthen bonds and create opportunities for connection.
- **Communicating Openly**: Be open and honest in your communication with others, expressing your thoughts, feelings, and needs clearly and respectfully. Relationships require effective communication to be built on mutual understanding and trust.
- **Showing Empathy**: Practice empathy by listening attentively to others, acknowledging their feelings, and showing understanding and compassion. Empathy helps foster deeper connections and strengthens interpersonal bonds.
- **Being Reliable**: Demonstrate reliability and dependability in your interactions with others by following through on commitments, being punctual, and offering support when needed. Reliability builds trust and confidence in relationships.

Effective Communication Skills

Effective communication is essential for successful social interactions and healthy relationships. For individuals with autism, who may struggle with verbal and nonverbal communication, learning effective communication skills is crucial for navigating social situations and expressing oneself clearly and confidently. Some effective communication skills that individuals with autism may find helpful include:

- **Active Listening**: Practice active listening by giving your full attention to the speaker, maintaining eye contact, and nodding or providing verbal cues to show that you're engaged and attentive.
- **Expressing Yourself Clearly**: Use clear, concise language to express your thoughts, feelings, and needs. Avoid using ambiguous or overly complex language that may be difficult for others to understand.
- **Nonverbal Communication**: Pay attention to your nonverbal cues, such as facial expressions, body language, and tone of voice, as these can convey important information and emotions to others. Practice using nonverbal cues effectively to enhance your communication skills.
- **Asking for Clarification**: If you're unsure about something or need more information, don't hesitate to ask for clarification. Asking questions demonstrates active engagement and shows that you're interested in understanding the other person's perspective.

Assertiveness Training

Assertiveness involves expressing your thoughts, feelings, and needs in a clear, direct, and respectful manner while also respecting the rights and boundaries of others. For individuals with autism, who may struggle with assertiveness and advocating for themselves in social situations, assertiveness training can be empowering and liberating. Some tips for developing assertiveness skills include:

- **Using "I" Statements**: Use "I" statements to express your thoughts, feelings, and needs assertively, rather than resorting to blaming or accusatory language. For example, say "I feel frustrated when..." rather than "You always..."
- **Setting Boundaries**: Establish clear boundaries in your relationships and communicate them assertively to others. Let others know what behaviors are acceptable and unacceptable to you, and be firm in enforcing your boundaries.
- **Practicing Assertive Body Language**: Use confident body language, such as maintaining good posture, making eye contact, and speaking clearly and calmly, to convey assertiveness and self-assurance.
- **Assertive Problem-Solving**: When conflicts arise, approach them assertively by calmly stating the issue, expressing your needs, and working together with the other person to find a mutually agreeable solution.

Setting Boundaries

Setting boundaries is essential for maintaining healthy relationships and protecting your emotional well-being. Boundaries help define acceptable behaviors, expectations, and limits in relationships, and they empower individuals to assert their needs and values. For individuals with autism, who may struggle with understanding and asserting boundaries, learning to set and maintain boundaries is crucial for establishing respectful and fulfilling relationships. Some tips for setting boundaries include:

- **Identifying Your Needs**: Take time to identify your needs, values, and priorities in relationships. Knowing what's important to you will help you establish clear boundaries and communicate them effectively to others.
- **Communicating Boundaries**: Clearly communicate your boundaries to others in a calm, assertive manner. Express your demands and expectations using "I" expressions, and be stern when enforcing your boundaries.
- **Respecting Others' Boundaries**: Respect the boundaries of others by listening to their needs and preferences, honoring their requests, and refraining from behaviors that violate their boundaries.
- **Reinforcing Boundaries**: Be consistent in enforcing your boundaries and addressing any violations that occur. Assertively assert your boundaries when necessary, and don't hesitate to remove yourself from situations or relationships that consistently disregard your boundaries.

By developing interpersonal effectiveness skills, individuals with autism can enhance their social competence, build stronger relationships, and navigate social interactions with greater confidence and ease. It's important to approach the process of building relationships and developing communication skills with patience, practice, and self-compassion, knowing that progress takes time and effort. With support and guidance, individuals with autism can cultivate meaningful connections and thrive in their interpersonal interactions.

6

Chapter 6

Core Mindfulness

C ore mindfulness is a fundamental aspect of Dialectical Behavior Therapy (DBT) that emphasizes the practice of being fully present in the moment with open awareness and acceptance. It involves developing skills for observing, describing, and participating in one's experiences without judgment or attachment. Core mindfulness techniques help individuals cultivate greater self-awareness, emotional regulation, and resilience in the face of life's challenges. By learning to engage with their thoughts, emotions, and sensations with curiosity and compassion, individuals can develop a deeper understanding of themselves and their inner experiences, leading to greater overall well-being.

Observing, Describing, and Participating

Observing, describing, and participating are three core mindfulness skills that form the foundation of DBT practice. These skills help individuals develop greater awareness and understanding of their inner experiences and the world around them.

- **Observing**: Observing involves paying attention to one's internal experiences, such as thoughts, emotions, bodily sensations, and external stimuli, without getting caught up in judgment or analysis. This skill allows individuals to simply notice their experiences as they arise, without trying to change or control them.
- **Describing**: Describing involves putting words to one's internal experiences, accurately and nonjudgmentally. This skill helps individuals develop a more precise and objective understanding of their thoughts, feelings, and sensations, which can facilitate greater self-awareness and communication with others.
- **Participating**: Participating involves fully engaging in the present moment and actively participating in one's experiences. This skill encourages individuals to immerse themselves in their activities and interactions with a sense of openness, curiosity, and commitment.

Practicing observing, describing, and participating can help individuals develop greater mindfulness and awareness in their daily lives, leading to increased emotional regulation, stress reduction, and overall well-being.

Non-judgmental Stance

A non-judgmental stance is a key aspect of mindfulness practice that involves approaching one's experiences with acceptance, openness, and compassion. Rather than evaluating or criticizing one's thoughts, feelings, or behaviors as "good" or "bad," a non-judgmental stance encourages individuals to simply observe and accept their experiences as they are, without trying to change or control them. This attitude of non-judgmental acceptance allows individuals to cultivate greater self-compassion, reduce self-criticism, and develop a more balanced and compassionate relationship with themselves and others.

Practicing a non-judgmental stance involves:

- **Cultivating Awareness**: Become aware of your judgments and evaluations of yourself and others, and practice letting go of these judgments with mindfulness and self-compassion.
- **Developing Compassion**: Practice self-compassion by offering yourself kindness and understanding in moments of difficulty or distress. Treat yourself with the same compassion and acceptance that you would offer to a friend in need.
- **Accepting Imperfection**: Embrace the reality of human imperfection and recognize that making mistakes and experiencing difficulties are natural and unavoidable parts of life. Practice accepting yourself and others as imperfect beings deserving of love and compassion.

One-mindfully

One-mindfully is a mindfulness skill that involves focusing one's attention and energy on a single task or activity at a time, with full concentration and commitment. Rather than multi-tasking or splitting attention between multiple activities, one-mindfulness encourages individuals to immerse themselves fully in the present moment and give their full attention to whatever they are doing. This focused attention can help individuals cultivate greater clarity, efficiency, and effectiveness in their actions, leading to improved productivity and satisfaction in their daily lives.

Practicing one-mindfully involves:

- **Setting Priorities**: Identify your priorities and focus your attention on the most important tasks or activities at hand. Let go of distractions and avoid spreading yourself too thin by trying to do too many things at once.
- **Eliminating Distractions**: Minimize distractions in your environment, such as turning off electronic devices, closing unnecessary tabs or windows, and creating a quiet, clutter-free workspace.
- **Practicing Mindful Engagement**: Engage fully in whatever task or activity you are doing, bringing your full attention and energy to the present moment. Notice any distractions or wandering thoughts that arise and gently redirect your focus back to the task at hand.
- **Taking Breaks**: Take regular breaks to rest and recharge your energy, allowing yourself to step away from your work and come back to it with renewed focus and clarity.

Effectively

Effectively is a mindfulness skill that involves taking effective action to achieve one's goals and meet one's needs while maintaining self-respect and respecting the rights and boundaries of others. Effectiveness is about finding a balance between assertiveness and cooperation, and between short-term and long-term goals. By practicing effectiveness, individuals can learn to navigate interpersonal interactions and decision-making processes more skillfully, leading to greater success and satisfaction in their personal and professional lives.

Practicing effectively involves:

- **Clarifying Goals**: Clearly define your goals and priorities, and identify the steps needed to achieve them. Break larger goals down into smaller, manageable tasks, and create a plan for how to accomplish them effectively.
- **Considering Consequences**: Consider the potential consequences of your actions and decisions, both for yourself and for others. Choose actions that are likely to lead to positive outcomes and align with your values and priorities.
- **Asserting Yourself**: Assert yourself confidently and respectfully in interpersonal interactions, expressing your thoughts, feelings, and needs clearly and assertively. Advocate for yourself and communicate your boundaries and expectations with confidence.
- **Flexibility**: Remain flexible and adaptable in your approach, willing to adjust your strategies and plans as needed in response to changing circumstances or feedback from others. Be open to new ideas and perspectives, and willing to consider alternative solutions to challenges.

By practicing core mindfulness skills such as observing, de-scribing, participating, maintaining a non-judgmental stance, practicing one-mindfully, and acting effectively, individuals can cultivate greater self-awareness, emotional regulation, and interpersonal effectiveness, leading to improved overall well-being and success in their lives. It's important to ap-proach mindfulness practice with patience, persistence, and self-compassion, knowing that progress takes time and effort. With dedication and practice, individuals can develop valuable skills for navigating life's challenges with greater ease and resilience.

7

Chapter 7

Emotion Regulation

E motion regulation is the process of effectively managing and modulating one's emotional experiences
in order to adaptively respond to the demands of
different situations. It involves recognizing, understanding,
and accepting one's emotions, as well as employing strategies
to regulate them in healthy and constructive ways. Emotion
regulation is essential for promoting psychological well-being,
fostering resilience, and maintaining healthy relationships.
For individuals with autism, who may experience heightened
emotional sensitivity or difficulty regulating their emotions
in response to sensory stimuli, learning effective emotion
regulation skills is particularly important for promoting
emotional stability and overall quality of life.

Understanding Emotion Regulation

Emotion regulation involves a variety of cognitive, behavioral, and physiological processes that help individuals manage their emotions in different contexts. These processes include:

- **Emotional Awareness**: Recognizing and identifying one's emotions as they arise, including both positive and negative emotions.
- **Emotional Understanding**: Understanding the causes and consequences of one's emotions, as well as the ways in which emotions influence thoughts, behaviors, and relationships.
- **Emotion Acceptance**: Accepting and validating one's emotional experiences without judgment or criticism, recognizing that all emotions are valid and deserving of attention and respect.
- **Emotion Modulation**: Employing strategies to regulate the intensity, duration, and expression of one's emotions in order to achieve desired outcomes and maintain psychological well-being.

Strategies for Managing Emotions

There are various strategies that individuals can use to manage their emotions effectively:

- **Cognitive Strategies**: Cognitive strategies involve changing the way one thinks about a situation in order to alter emotional responses. This may include reframing negative thoughts, challenging cognitive distortions, and adopting more adaptive perspectives.

- **Behavioral Strategies**: Behavioral strategies involve changing one's actions or behaviors in order to influence emotional experiences. This may include engaging in activities that promote relaxation and stress reduction, such as exercise, hobbies, or spending time in nature.
- **Physiological Strategies**: Physiological strategies involve regulating physiological arousal in order to manage emotional experiences. Practices including progressive muscular relaxation, mindfulness meditation, and deep breathing techniques may be included.
- **Social Strategies**: Social strategies involve seeking support from others in order to cope with emotional distress. This may include talking to friends, family members, or mental health professionals, or engaging in support groups or therapy.

Identifying Triggers and Vulnerabilities

Identifying triggers and vulnerabilities is an important step in managing emotions effectively. Triggers are external or internal stimuli that provoke emotional reactions, while vulnerabilities are factors that increase the likelihood of experiencing intense or dysregulated emotions. By identifying triggers and vulnerabilities, individuals can become more aware of the situations, thoughts, and experiences that contribute to their emotional distress, allowing them to develop strategies for coping more effectively. Some common triggers and vulnerabilities may include:

- **Stressful Situations**: High-pressure or conflictual situations, such as work deadlines, relationship conflicts, or financial difficulties, can trigger emotional distress for many individuals.

- **Negative Thought Patterns**: Negative thought patterns, such as self-criticism, catastrophizing, or black-and-white thinking, can contribute to feelings of anxiety, depression, or anger.
- **Sensory Overload**: Individuals with autism may be particularly sensitive to sensory stimuli, such as loud noises, bright lights, or crowded environments, which can trigger emotional dysregulation.
- **Trauma or Past Experiences**: Past experiences of trauma or adversity can create vulnerabilities to experiencing intense emotions in similar situations in the future.

Building Positive Emotional Experiences:

Building positive emotional experiences is an important aspect of emotion regulation and overall well-being. Positive emotions play a crucial role in promoting resilience, enhancing social connections, and buffering against the negative effects of stress and adversity. Some strategies for building positive emotional experiences include:

- **Engaging in Pleasurable Activities**: Identify activities that bring joy, pleasure, and satisfaction, and make time for them regularly. This may include hobbies, creative pursuits, or spending time with loved ones.
- **Cultivating Gratitude**: Practice gratitude by focusing on the things you're thankful for in your life, whether big or small. Keeping a gratitude journal, expressing gratitude to others, or simply taking a moment to appreciate the beauty of the

present moment can help cultivate a sense of positivity and well-being.

· **Fostering Positive Relationships**: Nurture relationships with supportive friends, family members, and peers who uplift and inspire you. Spending time with loved ones, sharing meaningful experiences, and expressing affection and appreciation can enhance feelings of connection and belonging.

· **Mindfulness and Self-Compassion**: Practice mindfulness and self-compassion by bringing awareness to your present-moment experiences with openness and acceptance, and treating yourself with kindness and understanding in moments of difficulty or distress.

By understanding the principles of emotion regulation, learning effective strategies for managing emotions, identifying triggers and vulnerabilities, and building positive emotional experiences, individuals can enhance their emotional resilience, reduce emotional distress, and improve their overall quality of life. It's important to approach the process of emotion regulation with patience, self-compassion, and a willingness to experiment with different techniques to find what works best for you. With practice and persistence, individuals can develop valuable skills for navigating the complexities of human emotions with greater ease and confidence.

8

Chapter 8

Walking the Middle Path

Walking the middle path is a core principle of Dialectical Behavior Therapy (DBT) that emphasizes finding balance between opposing forces such as acceptance and change, validation and problem-solving, and self-compassion and personal growth. It involves recognizing and honoring the dialectical nature of life, where two seemingly contradictory truths can coexist simultaneously. For individuals with autism, who may experience difficulties with flexibility, rigidity in thinking, and black-and-white thinking, learning to walk the middle path can be particularly valuable for fostering resilience, enhancing emotional regulation, and promoting overall well-being.

Balancing Acceptance and Change

Balancing acceptance and change involves finding a middle ground between accepting things as they are and actively working towards change. This dialectical approach recognizes that while acceptance is important for cultivating inner peace and well-being, change is often necessary for personal growth and fulfillment. Some strategies for balancing acceptance and change include:

- **Radical Acceptance**: Practice radical acceptance by fully accepting reality as it is, without judgment or resistance. This doesn't mean condoning or approving of difficult situations or painful emotions, but rather acknowledging them as they are without trying to change or control them.
- **Mindful Action**: Strive for positive change in your life by taking conscious, purposeful action, and by remaining accepting and nonjudgmental of others and yourself. This involves being present and mindful in your actions, and making choices that align with your values and goals.
- **Cultivating Flexibility**: Develop flexibility in your thinking and behavior by being open to new perspectives, willing to adapt to changing circumstances, and embracing uncertainty and ambiguity with curiosity and resilience.
- **Finding Balance**: Strive to find a balance between acceptance and change that feels authentic and sustainable for you. This may involve setting realistic goals, prioritizing self-care, and being gentle with yourself during times of transition or challenge.

Finding Middle Ground

Finding middle ground involves seeking compromise and reso-
lution in interpersonal conflicts and navigating the complexities
of relationships. It requires recognizing and validating both
your own needs and the needs of others, and working towards
mutually satisfactory solutions. Some strategies for finding
middle ground include:

- **Active Listening**: Practice active listening by paying attention to the perspectives and feelings of others, and
  validating their experiences without judgment or criticism.
  Demonstrate empathy and understanding by reflecting
  back what you hear and acknowledging the validity of their
  emotions.
- **Collaborative Problem-Solving**: Approach conflicts and
  disagreements as opportunities for collaboration and
  growth, rather than competition or confrontation. Seek
  win-win solutions that address the needs and concerns
  of all parties involved, and be willing to compromise and
  negotiate to find common ground.
- **Respecting Boundaries**: Respect the boundaries and au-
  tonomy of others by honoring their preferences, values,
  and personal space. Communicate openly and respectfully,
  and be willing to adjust your behavior or expectations in
  response to feedback from others.
- **Finding Shared Values**: Identify shared values and goals
  that you have in common with others, and use them as
  a foundation for building understanding and connection.
  Focus on areas of agreement and common ground, rather
  than differences and disagreements.

Radical Acceptance

Radical acceptance is the practice of fully accepting reality as it is, without judgment or resistance. It entails being open-minded and compassionate while accepting the present moment and all of its experiences, whether good and bad. Radical acceptance does not mean giving up or resigning oneself to suffering, but rather recognizing that resisting reality only leads to greater emotional distress and suffering. Some strategies for practicing radical acceptance include:

- **Mindfulness**: Cultivate mindfulness by bringing awareness to your present-moment experiences with openness, curiosity, and non-judgment. Notice any resistance or aversion that arises, and practice letting go of the need to control or change reality.
- **Self-Compassion**: Offer yourself kindness and understanding in moments of difficulty or distress, recognizing that suffering is a natural part of the human experience. Treat yourself with the same compassion and acceptance that you would offer to a friend in need.
- **Letting Go of Control**: Give up trying to influence or alter situations that are out of your control and concentrate on the response you decide to give them. Surrender to the flow of life and trust in your ability to cope and adapt to whatever arises.
- **Finding Meaning**: Find meaning and purpose in your experiences, even in the face of adversity or suffering. Look for opportunities for growth, learning, and connection, and recognize that challenges can be valuable opportunities for personal and spiritual development.

42

Finding Meaning and Purpose

Finding meaning and purpose involves identifying what matters most to you in life and aligning your actions and goals with your values and aspirations. It's about cultivating a sense of meaning, fulfillment, and connection to something greater than yourself, whether it be through relationships, work, hobbies, or spiritual practices. Some strategies for finding meaning and purpose include:

- **Clarifying Values**: Take time to reflect on your values, beliefs, and priorities, and identify what truly matters most to you in life. Consider what brings you joy, fulfillment, and a sense of purpose, and use this as a guide for making decisions and setting goals.
- **Setting Meaningful Goals**: Set goals that are aligned with your values and aspirations, and that contribute to your sense of meaning and purpose. Dictate more ambitious objectives into more doable milestones, and acknowledge and appreciate your advancements as you go.
- **Cultivating Connection**: Cultivate meaningful connections with others by nurturing relationships with friends, family members, and community members who support and inspire you. Share your experiences, thoughts, and feelings with others, and seek opportunities for collaboration and mutual growth.
- **Engaging in Meaningful Activities**: Engage in activities that bring you a sense of joy, fulfillment, and connection, whether it be through creative expression, volunteering, or pursuing hobbies and interests that you're passionate about.

43

By practicing the principles of walking the middle path, balancing acceptance and change, finding middle ground, radical acceptance, and finding meaning and purpose, individuals can cultivate greater resilience, emotional well-being, and fulfillment in their lives. It's important to approach these practices with patience, openness, and self-compassion, knowing that progress takes time and effort. With dedication and practice, individuals can develop valuable skills for navigating life's challenges with greater ease and resilience.

9

Chapter 9

Putting It All Together

The process of Dialectical Behavior Therapy (DBT) culminates at a place where clients integrate and put the abilities they've acquired along the way—such as emotional control, interpersonal effectiveness, and general well-being—into practice.This phase involves reviewing the skills learned, creating a personalized DBT plan, and moving forward with confidence to navigate life's challenges with resilience and self-assurance.

Review of Skills Learned

Before moving forward, it's essential to review the skills learned during DBT therapy. This review serves as a reminder of the progress made and the tools available for managing emotions, navigating relationships, and fostering personal growth. Key skills to review may include:

- **Mindfulness Techniques**: Reflect on the mindfulness exercises practiced, such as observing, describing, and participating, as well as mindfulness of emotions and thoughts.
- **Emotion Regulation Strategies**: Review the various emotion regulation techniques explored, including identifying and labeling emotions, understanding triggers and vulnerabilities, and implementing distress tolerance skills.
- **Interpersonal Effectiveness Skills**: Consider the interpersonal effectiveness skills learned, such as effective communication, assertiveness training, setting boundaries, and finding middle ground in relationships.
- **Distress Tolerance Techniques**: Reflect on the distress tolerance skills acquired, such as coping with intense emotions, crisis survival skills, distracting techniques, and self-soothing strategies.

By reviewing these skills, individuals can reinforce their understanding and application, ensuring they are equipped to handle life's challenges effectively.

Creating a Personalized DBT Plan

After reviewing the skills learned, individuals can create a personalized DBT plan tailored to their unique needs, goals, and preferences. This plan serves as a roadmap for ongoing growth and development, outlining specific strategies and interventions to support emotional regulation, interpersonal effectiveness, and overall well-being. When creating a personalized DBT plan, consider the following steps:

1. **Identify Goals:** Clarify your short-term and long-term goals, both in terms of emotional well-being and personal development. These goals may include improving emotional regulation, enhancing relationships, reducing stress, or pursuing meaningful activities.

2. **Assess Strengths and Areas for Growth**: Reflect on your strengths and areas for growth, considering your past experiences, challenges, and successes. Identify the skills and qualities that have served you well, as well as areas where you may benefit from additional support or development.

3. **Select Relevant Skills**: Choose specific DBT skills and techniques that align with your goals and areas for growth. Consider which skills are most relevant to your current challenges and priorities, and prioritize those for inclusion in your plan.

4. **Develop Action Steps**: Break down each skill into actionable steps or strategies that you can implement in your daily life. Consider how you will practice and integrate each skill into your routines and interactions, and identify any potential obstacles or barriers that may arise.

5. **Set Milestones and Tracking Measures**: Establish milestones and tracking measures to monitor your progress and evaluate the effectiveness of your DBT plan. Set specific goals and timelines for achieving desired outcomes, and track your progress regularly to ensure you're on track toward your objectives.

6. **Seek Support and Accountability**: Engage the support of a therapist, counselor, or support group to provide guidance, encouragement, and accountability as you work toward

your goals. Share your DBT plan with trusted individuals who can offer support and feedback along the way.

Moving Forward with Confidence

With a personalized DBT plan in place, individuals can move forward with confidence, knowing they have the tools and support needed to navigate life's challenges effectively. Moving forward with confidence involves:

- **Commitment to Practice**: Dedicate yourself to regular practice and implementation of DBT skills in your daily life. Consistent practice is key to building competency and confidence in using these skills to manage emotions, navigate relationships, and promote well-being.
- **Flexibility and Adaptability**: Remain open to learning and growth, and be willing to adapt your approach as needed based on feedback and experience. Embrace challenges as opportunities for learning and development, and approach setbacks with resilience and determination.
- **Celebrating Progress**: Acknowledge and celebrate your progress and achievements along the way, no matter how small. Recognize the efforts you've made and the positive changes you've experienced as a result of your commitment to DBT practice.
- **Self-Compassion**: Practice self-compassion and kindness toward yourself, especially during times of difficulty or setback. As you would a buddy going through a similar situation, show yourself the same compassion and under-standing.
- **Seeking Support**: Reach out for support and guidance when

needed, whether from a therapist, counselor, support group, or trusted friend or family member. Remember that you're not alone on this journey, and there are people who care about you and want to see you succeed.

By putting it all together, individuals can harness the transformative power of Dialectical Behavior Therapy to cultivate greater resilience, emotional well-being, and personal growth. With a personalized DBT plan, commitment to practice, and support from others, individuals can navigate life's challenges with confidence, courage, and resilience, knowing they have the skills and resources needed to thrive.

Conclusion

In conclusion, Dialectical Behavior Therapy (DBT) offers a comprehensive and effective approach to promoting emotional regulation, interpersonal effectiveness, and overall well-being for individuals facing a variety of challenges, including autism. Throughout this workbook, we have explored key DBT principles and techniques aimed at helping individuals develop essential skills for managing emotions, navigating relationships, and fostering personal growth.

From understanding emotions and practicing mindfulness to building distress tolerance and interpersonal effectiveness, each chapter has provided valuable insights and practical strategies for enhancing emotional resilience and promoting positive change. By incorporating mindfulness practices, learning to regulate emotions, and developing effective communication skills, individuals can cultivate greater self-awareness, improve relationships, and experience greater overall satisfaction and fulfillment in their lives.

The journey through this DBT workbook has been one of self-discovery, growth, and empowerment. By applying the principles and techniques learned, individuals can move forward with confidence, knowing they have the tools and resources needed to navigate life's challenges with resilience and grace. Whether facing moments of emotional turmoil, interpersonal conflict, or existential uncertainty, individuals can draw upon the skills and insights gained from DBT to navigate the complexities of life with greater ease and confidence.

As individuals continue on their journey of self-discovery and personal growth, it's important to remember that progress takes time and effort. It's okay to encounter setbacks and challenges along the way – what matters most is the commitment to learning, growing, and striving for greater well-being. By embracing the principles of DBT – acceptance, mindfulness, and effective action – individuals can cultivate a deeper sense of meaning, purpose, and fulfillment in their lives, ultimately leading to greater happiness and well-being.